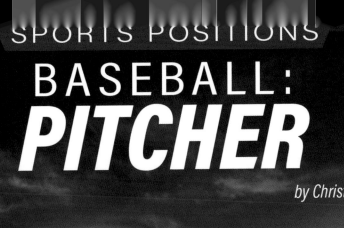

SPORTS POSITIONS

BASEBALL:
PITCHER

by Christina Earley

A Stingray Book

SEAHORSE
PUBLISHING

Teaching Tips for Caregivers and Teachers:

This Hi-Lo book features high-interest subject matter that will appeal to all readers in intermediate and middle school grades. It may be enjoyed by students reading at or above grade level as well as by those who are looking for age-appropriate themes matched with a less challenging reading level. Hi-Lo books are ideal for ELL readers, too.

Each book appeals to a striving reader's age and maturity level. Opportunities are provided for students to read words they already know while encountering a limited number of new, high-interest vocabulary words. With these supports in place, students will read more fluently while increasing reading comprehension. Use the following suggestions to help students grow as readers.

- Encourage the student to read independently at home.
- Encourage the student to practice reading aloud.
- Encourage activities that require reading.
- Establish a regular reading time.
- Have the student write questions about what they read.

Teaching Tips for Teachers:

Before Reading
- Ask, "What do I know about this topic?"
- Ask, "What do I want to learn about this topic?"

During Reading
- Ask, "What is the author trying to teach me?"
- Ask, "How is this like something I already know?"

After Reading
- Discuss how the text features (headings, index, etc.) help with understanding the topic.
- Ask, "What interesting or fun fact did you learn?"

TABLE OF CONTENTS

WHAT IS A PITCHER?

Pitcher is a position on a baseball team.

Pitchers are members of the defense, or non-scoring part of the team.

They **pitch** the ball to the batter on the opposing team.

The pitcher wants the batter to get a **strikeout**.

FUN FACT

In the National League of Major League Baseball, pitchers also hit.

jersey

pants

stockings

UNIFORM

Baseball shirts, or jerseys, have the name and number of the player.

Pants and **stockings** complete the bottom of the uniform.

Caps with brims are worn to keep the sun out of the eyes.

A special glove is smaller and blocks the view of the grip of the ball.

BEFORE THE GAME

Pitchers exercise to build arm, leg, and core muscles.

They practice throwing the ball with **accuracy**.

Working with coaches helps pitchers get better.

Eating healthy food makes sure pitchers are strong and have energy.

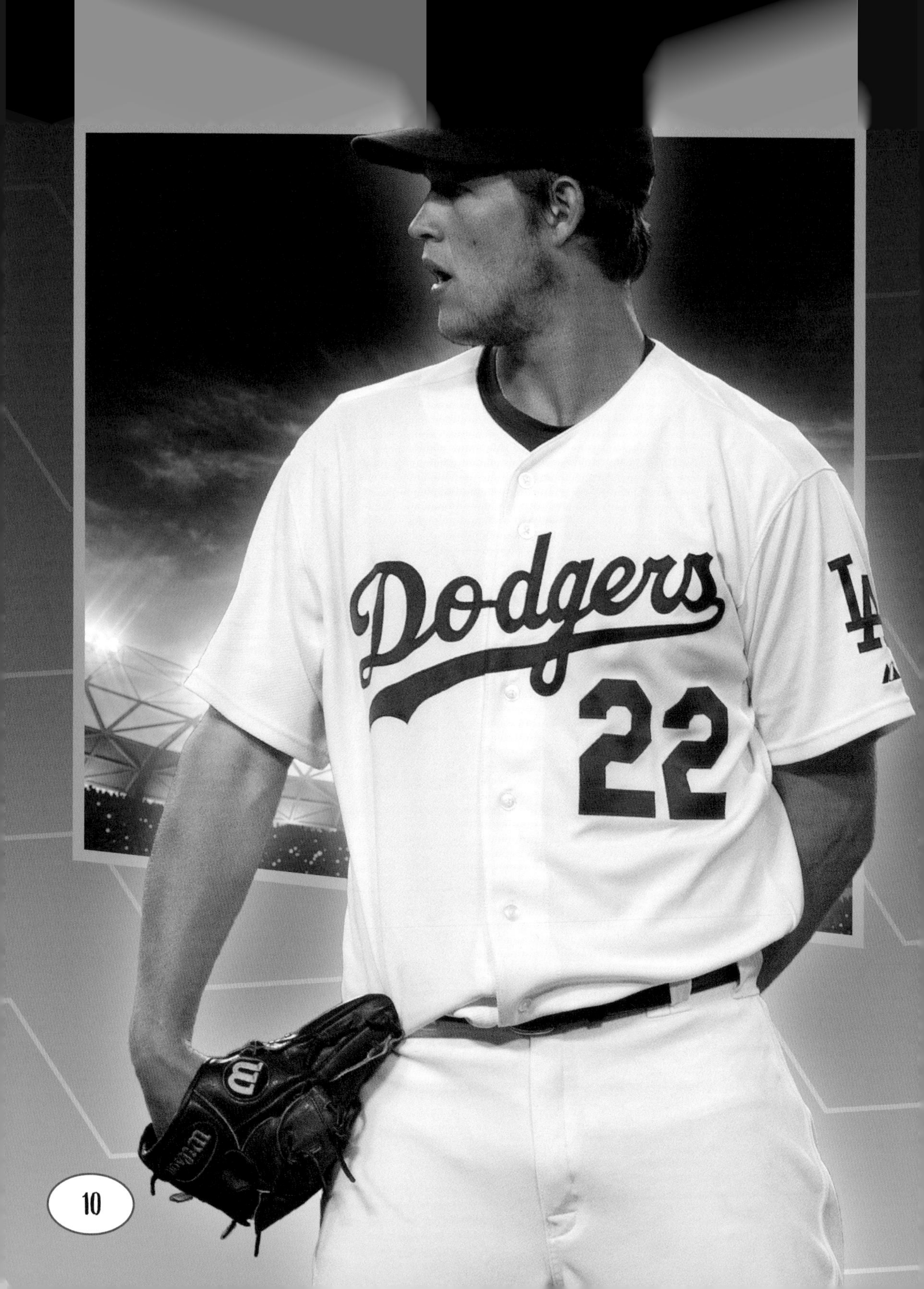
Dodgers
22
LA

DURING THE GAME

The pitcher stands on the pitcher's mound to throw the ball to the batter.

When a ball is coming up the middle, the pitcher will **field** the ball.

Sometimes, the pitcher has to run to first base before the batter gets there.

Watching the batters helps the pitcher know what pitch to use to get the player to strike out.

FUN FACT

Sometimes, pitchers go to first base to cover for the first baseman.

TYPES OF PITCHERS

The best pitcher, or ace, usually starts the **rotation**.

Relief pitchers start to throw practice balls when the current pitcher is tired.

The closer is saved for the last inning of a game when the team is in the lead.

FUN FACT

"We will land on the moon before I hit a home run," said San Francisco Giants pitcher Gaylord Perry. Twenty minutes after Neil Armstrong landed on the moon, Perry hit a home run.

HISTORY

The first rules for baseball were written in 1845.

One of the rules said the ball was to be pitched, or thrown underhand, to the batter.

In the 1870s, the pitcher used different pitches to make it harder for the batter to hit the ball.

FUN FACT

Jim Creighton was the first pitcher to add spin to the ball.

TRAITS OF A GREAT PITCHER

Great pitchers can throw a ball with **velocity**, or speed.

They pitch the ball with accuracy.

These players are able to concentrate and focus during tough games.

Pitchers keep learning how to improve.

NOTES FROM THE COACH

- Be a leader on and off the field.

- Listen and take constructive criticism from coaches and teammates.

- Admit mistakes and improve.

- Have **grit** to never give up even when things are tough.

- Learn all parts of the game and all positions.

- Work hard during practices and in games.

- Eat a well-balanced diet.

- Have a good attitude and be respectful to others.

DENNIS ECKERSLEY
- World Series champion 1989
- American League MVP 1992
- Cy Young Award 1992
- Fifth place for games played with 1,071

ROLLIE FINGERS
- American League MVP 1981
- Cy Young Award 1981
- Four-time Rolaids Relief winner 1977, 1978, 1980, 1981
- World Series champion 1972, 1973, 1974

TREVOR HOFFMAN
- Second place for career saves with 601
- Two-time Rolaids Relief winner 1998, 2006
- Second place for career games finished with 856
- Seven All-Star games

RANDY JOHNSON
- Triple Crown winner 2002
- Cy Young Award 1995, 1999, 2000, 2001, 2002
- World Series champion 2001
- Six-time WAR leader 1995, 1999, 2000, 2001, 2002, 2004

CLAYTON KERSHAW
- World Series champion 2020
- Cy Young Award 2011, 2013, 2014
- National League MVP 2014
- Triple Crown winner 2011

SANDY KOUFAX
- National League MVP 1963
- World Series champion 1959, 1963, 1965
- Cy Young Award 1963, 1965, 1966
- Triple Crown winner 1963, 1965, 1966

PEDRO MARTINEZ
- Three-time WAR leader 1997, 1999, 2000
- World Series champion 2004
- Cy Young Award 1997, 1999, 2000
- Five-time ERA leader 1997, 1999, 2000, 2002, 2003

MARIANO RIVERA
- Five-time Rolaids Relief winner 1999, 2001, 2004, 2005, 2009
- World Series champion 1996, 1998, 1999, 2000, 2009
- First place in career games finished with 952
- First place in career saves with 652

HOYT WILHELM
- ERA leader 1952, 1959
- Sixth place in career games played with 1,070
- 1954 World Series champion
- Career WHIP of 1.125

CY YOUNG
- World Series champion 1903
- Most wins by a pitcher in a career with 511
- ERA leader 1892, 1901
- Triple Crown winner 1901

GLOSSARY

accuracy (A·kyoo·ruh·see): precision or correctness

field (feeld): to scoop up a ball that was hit or thrown to you

grit (grit): courage and strength of character

pitch (pich): to throw the ball for the batter to try to hit

rotation (roh·TAY·shuhn): the group of starting pitchers for a team

stockings (STAH·kingz): long socks worn by men

strikeout (STRIGHK·out): an out called when a batter accumulates three strikes

velocity (vuh·LOS·i·tee): the speed of something in a given direction

INDEX

AFTER READING QUESTIONS

1. What do pitchers practice the most?

2. What pitcher is used in the last inning of the game?

3. How were pitchers supposed to throw according to the original rules?

About the Author

Christina Earley lives in sunny Florida with her husband and son. She has always loved different sports. She enjoys traveling to see different stadiums, arenas, and ballparks where she always has to eat the local hot dog.

Written by: Christina Earley
Design by: Kathy Walsh
Editor: Kim Thompson

Library of Congress PCN Data
Baseball: Pitcher / Christina Earley
Sports Positions
ISBN 978-1-63897-105-4 (hard cover)
ISBN 978-1-63897-191-7 (paperback)
ISBN 978-1-63897-277-8 (EPUB)
ISBN 978-1-63897-363-8 (eBook)
Library of Congress Control Number: 2021945196

Printed in the United States of America.

Photographs/Shutterstock: Cover, Pg 1, ©Debby Wong: Cover, P 3-22 ©ExpressVectors: Cover Pg 5, 6, 9, 10, 11, 14, 17, 18 ©Eugene Onischenko: Pg 5 ©Photo Works: Pg 6 ©Bill Florence: Pg 9 ©Debby Wong: Pg 10 ©Photo Works: Pg 13 ©sirtravelalot: Pg 14©PD: Pg 17 Keith Allison @ Wikif: Pg 18 ©Debby Wong: Pg 23 ©Master1305

Seahorse Publishing Company

www.seahorsepub.com

Published in the United States
Seahorse Publishing
PO Box 771325
Coral Springs, FL 33077